Body and Soul

Body
and
Soul

John Mighton

Coach House Press
Toronto

Coach House Press
50 Prince Arthur Avenue, Suite 107
Toronto, Canada

© John Mighton, 1994

FIRST EDITION
Printed in Canada

Published with the assistance of the Canada Council, the Ontario Arts
Council, the Department of Canadian Heritage and the Ontario Publishing
Centre.

Canadian Cataloguing in Publication Data

Mighton, John, 1957 —
  Body and soul

A play.
ISBN 0-88910-474-3

I. Title.

PS8576.I29B6 1994   C812'.54   C94-930661-4
PR9199.3.M54B6 1994

Contents

Introduction

What is John Mighton's play, *Body and Soul,* all about: desire, sex, virtual reality, mass media, non-communication?

In a manner that at times recalls Chekhov, and at other times Brecht, Mighton alludes to all of these subjects in his portrayal of our times, when visual communication has substantially displaced verbal communication. His characters provide a picture of a pervasive mediocrity which does not realize that our senses are lulled by what one character calls 'too much information', or that the 'techniques of arguing' are so skilfully developed that we do not recognize how fatefully they shape our lives, in which everything is reduced to a commodity to sell—be it a politician, a car, sex, or a donut.

If, as Marshall McLuhan said, 'the medium is the message', then Mighton's 'message' is that our addiction to technology and visual images may have already paved the way for our enslavement to constantly created new desires. As Mighton himself has said in an interview, 'desire depends on some kind of taboo or resistance. You always want something that is inaccessible. If technology makes it possible to satisfy all our desires, it may fragment things even further, make desire personal, less constrained by social mores and more inaccesssible to anyone else. People will be even less able to understand each other. We may lose the common language that keeps society together'. This loss of a common language and the replacement of a common value system with the artificially created desire for something else, results in insecurity, loneliness, and finally, virtual rather than actual communication.

Mighton opens the play with an interesting dramaturgical device: a love scene between Jane—an undertaker—and a corpse. (It ends that way too—though more ambiguously.) What is the difference between necrophilia and technophilia, which produces virtual reality? The first touches a societal taboo, while the latter—arguably as soulless and dead as a corpse—is acceptable. Jane's brother-in-law Henry ends up making love to a virtual woman via computer (operated by a co-operative man), and her sister Sally compensates for losing Henry by keeping company with an 'easily satisfied' dog. The 'significant other' is reduced to a machine, a corpse, or a dog. Does virtual communication mark a new phase in human development—as the scientist argues in Scene Eight—or the end of real communication?

Once hailed as a liberator of human nature, science has not only had a devastating effect on human relationships, it has also altered nature itself. Various characters tell us that 'dogs commit suicide', 'birds are flying into people's windows', and we have all read how ducks in Canada change their sex and stop breeding as a result of pollution.

With subject matter like this, one might expect the play to be depressing, yet *Body and Soul* is a very entertaining play indeed. In true Brechtian fashion, Mighton infuses his scenes with a sense of humour, irony, contradictions, and *Verfremdungseffekte.* Why is the necrophiliac, for instance, a woman, rather than a man? And who would expect a corpse to take the initiative? He turns Scene Six into a talk show about a man who wrote a book called *Unreal Estate:* it becomes a hilarious cabaret scene in which Mighton ridicules the extent to which we fail to analyze how news, advertising, or insidious propaganda manipulate our lives.

Presented in these Brechtian terms, but with an admixture of Chekhovian humanity—evident in the characters' struggles to transcend their lives—the sombre theme of the devastating separation of body and soul is both entertaining and instructive.

Pia Kleber, Toronto, 1994

Body and Soul

Production History

Body and Soul was first presented as part of the Atelier Work-shop programme by the National Arts Centre, Ottawa, in November 1993.

Director: Michael Devine
Set and Lighting Design: Robert Reid
Sound Design: Marc Desormeaux
Costume Co-ordination: Normand Thériault
Assistant Director: Linda McLachlan
Stage Manager: Mary Ellis
Cast: Marcel Jeannin, Catherine MacKenzie, Paul Rainville, Tennyson, Beverley Wolfe, with John Gordon and Marguerite Padlewska

Body and Soul premiered in a production by Theatre Passe Muraille and Crow's Theatre, Toronto, March 1994.

Director: Diane Cave
Composer/Sound Design: Brad Hilliker
Set and Lighting Design: Steve Lucas
Costume Design: Wendy White
Stage Manager: Winston Morgan
Production Manager: Andrea Lundy
Dramaturge: Raegan Mighton
Choreographer: Eryn Dace Trudell
Props: Andrew Bolton
Cast: Maggie Huculak, Randy Hughson, Nadia Ross, Andrew Scorer, Jane Spidell, with Eryn Dace Trudell and David Baile

Characters

JANE

MARK

HENRY

SALLY

MARY

Other roles may be doubled by the actors playing **MARK** and **MARY**.

Scene One

JANE *applies make-up to a corpse.* MARK *stands nearby*

MARK Want me to walk you home?

JANE No.

MARK How long before you're done?

JANE Half an hour.

MARK I don't mind waiting.

JANE That's all right.

[*Pause*]

MARK I read in the paper yesterday a dog committed suicide
by jumping off a bridge. First known case of canine suicide.

JANE How do they know it was suicide?

MARK There's no other explanation. It just walked up to the
edge and jumped. Its owner said it seemed depressed for
weeks … What would a dog have to be depressed about?

JANE It's not something you could ever understand.

MARK Why not?

JANE Because you're not a dog.

MARK You're right.

[*Pause*]

Mr. Wilson said you were here until twelve the other night.

JANE So?

MARK That's the third time this month.

JANE Have they put you on accounts or something?

MARK I'm just worried about you. All you do is work.

JANE I'm fine. You don't have to hang around for me.

MARK I was thinking about going to a party later. You want
to come?

JANE No thanks.

MARK Why not?

JANE I'm just not feeling very social.

MARK Are you seeing anyone?

JANE No.

MARK People have started to talk about you.

JANE What do they say?

MARK That you think you're too good for everyone.

JANE I am.

MARK You should come out with me some time. We'd have fun. We have a lot in common. I don't feel comfortable around people either. But I can talk to you. We understand each other.

[*Pause*]

Did you use the new lip sealant?

JANE Yes.

MARK It'll keep the colour from straying and feathering.

JANE I know.

[*Pause*]

MARK You've made him look beautiful. He must be twenty years old. How did he die?

JANE Drank wood alcohol.

MARK Why?

JANE How should I know?

[*Pause*]

MARK You see I feel that only someone like you could understand me. I'm very complicated. I've always ...

JANE Please stop talking!

[*Pause*]

MARK All right.

JANE I'm sorry ... It's hard to concentrate. I'm not doing a very good job.

MARK I guess I should leave you alone.

JANE I'll call you later. Maybe I'll go to that party.

MARK I think it would do you some good.

[*Pause*]

You'll lock the office?

JANE Yes.

MARK Maybe I'll see you later.

JANE Yes.

[MARK *exits.* JANE *bends and kisses the body. It embraces her*]

Scene Two

HENRY *sits reading an entertainment weekly.* SALLY *sits nearby*

HENRY Another dog died.

SALLY What?

HENRY There's a wave of dog suicides in San Francisco. And birds are flying into people's windows in New York and Halifax. They don't know what's causing it.

SALLY That's strange.

[*Pause.* HENRY *turns to the back of the paper*]

Next Friday is our anniversary.

HENRY Yes.

SALLY Are you glad we got married?

HENRY Yes.

SALLY When we met you said you wanted your freedom.

HENRY That was when we met.

SALLY Don't you ever feel restless?

HENRY No.

[*Pause*]

SALLY Why do you always read the ads at the back of that paper?

HENRY They're funny.

SALLY You spend hours reading them.

HENRY I told you—I find them amusing.

SALLY I find them depressing. There are so many strange people out there.

[*Pause. She begins to read over his shoulder*]

What's teledildonics?

HENRY The study of computer-generated images used for sex. Simulated sex.

SALLY I can't believe the government is funding that sort

16

of thing.

HENRY They want twenty volunteers. Maybe I'll try it.

SALLY Are you serious?

HENRY It's on the cutting edge. I may write an article about it.
[*Pause*]

SALLY I'm worried about you, Henry.

HENRY Why?

SALLY I've noticed you do nothing but read and talk about
sex lately.

HENRY Are you insane?

SALLY Even last night lying beside me in bed you were reading about sex.

HENRY I was reading the Buddhist scriptures for God's sake!

SALLY Yes, but I noticed the passage you underlined.

HENRY Now you're spying on me!

SALLY I'm just interested in what interests you. Maybe you
could tell me what this means: [*reading from the Buddhist
scriptures*] And Nanda looked at Indra's Grove, in all
directions, with eyes wide open and astonished. And the
celestial nymphs exuberantly came round him and eyed
each other in high spirits. When he saw that world to be
one long round of merry-making, and that no tiredness,
sleepiness, discontent, sorrow or disease existed anywhere,
the world of men seemed no better than a cemetery. Just as
the sun, when it rises, eclipses the lamp lit when it is dark,
so the glory of the celestial nymphs nullifies the lustre of all
merely human women.
[*Pause*]

HENRY It's a metaphor.

SALLY For what?

HENRY You've missed the point of the passage.

SALLY Which is?

HENRY If you'd bothered to read on it says that paradise is
illusory.

SALLY You didn't underline that part.

HENRY Look, when I first met you I was very immature. I felt
I had to prove myself sexually with everyone. But now I
realize there are more important things. That passage just
expresses the kind of hedonism I used to be into.
[*Pause*]

SALLY Am I that ugly?

HENRY You're beautiful.

SALLY Why can't you be happy with what you have. Too
many people spend their lives searching for something they
don't need in the first place. It should be so easy to be
happy.

HENRY I am happy.
[*He kisses her. She embraces him*]

Scene Three

JANE *places flowers on a grave.* MARY *approaches*

MARY Hello.
  [*Pause*]
  I'm Paul's mother.
  [*Pause*]
  Your flowers are beautiful.
JANE I was just leaving.
MARY Do you need a ride?
JANE No—I live near here.
MARY What's your name?
JANE Jane.
MARY Were you a friend?
JANE Yes.
MARY Paul never mentioned you.
JANE We met recently.
MARY I've seen you somewhere before.
JANE I was at the funeral.
MARY Oh yes … Paul was extremely shy around women. I
  didn't know he had any female friends. I tried not to
  interfere with his life. He was free to see whoever he
  wanted. I wasn't one of those domineering mothers.
  [*Pause*]
  Did he ever talk about me?
JANE Not to me.
MARY What about his father?
JANE No.
MARY In my day men loved women for what they'd been—
  for their youth and beauty. And women loved men for
  what they were going to be—for their success and power.

19

So there was never much time for them to be happy together.

JANE Your husband left you?

MARY Didn't Paul tell you?

JANE No.

MARY That's strange—Paul was never the same after that. My husband moved in with another woman. Paul thought I'd driven him away.

JANE My father left too. When I was twelve.

[Pause]

The men came and went, but the women were always there.

[Pause]

How old are you?

MARY Forty.

JANE You're beautiful.

MARY Thank you ... It was nice of you to bring flowers. You must have been very close. I'm glad Paul had one good friend.

JANE We were lovers.

[Pause]

MARY My son was gay.

[Pause]

I know you. You work at the funeral home. You didn't know my son.

[Pause]

What are you doing here? Why did you bring flowers?

[JANE exits]

What have you done to my son? Stay away from my son!

Scene Four

HENRY What do you think of my wife?

DOCTOR I hardly know her.

HENRY Do you think she's beautiful?

DOCTOR Yes, of course. Don't you?

HENRY Yes. She's the most beautiful woman I know.
[*Pause*]
I don't know what's wrong with me, doctor.

DOCTOR What do you mean?

HENRY I love my wife, but sometimes I feel like I'm being
torn apart. I have no direction in life. I go through each
day feeling like a slave to the world around me.

DOCTOR Have you been meditating?

HENRY Yes, but it's not working.

DOCTOR Contemplating the body in the proper way can free
us from the desires of the flesh.

HENRY I'm not sure it's a sexual thing.

DOCTOR Meditating on the skin, tissues, bones, sweat, bile,
phlegm, snot, blood and pus helps us discover that live
bodies and dead bodies differ only in degree.

HENRY Yes, but is it healthy?

DOCTOR Of course.

HENRY We all have natural urges.

DOCTOR We all feel hunger in the same way. But not desire.
It's not the same kind of instinct. That's because it involves
the imagination.

HENRY Regarding women as more or less the same as corpses
doesn't seem all that healthy to me.

DOCTOR Try it. Remember, you're not a pig. You're a god.
[*As the* DOCTOR *speaks he moves towards the front of the
stage. A light grows behind him until he is only seen in*

silhouette. Faintly we hear music and the sound of people moaning]

When you die you'll miss your body at first. You'll feel like a shadow squeezed into a crack between rocks. All around you, you'll be aware of humans and animals copulating. If the thought attracts you, if you long to re-enter a body, you'll be lost. At that moment a light will appear to guide you. No matter how much it hurts, you must follow that light. Give up all belief in a separate self, immerse yourself in the light, recognize this boundless light as your true self and you will be saved.

[*The lights return to normal and the music stops abruptly*]

I'm afraid our time is up. How's next Thursday at three?

HENRY Fine.

Scene Five

HENRY *sits reading the paper*

HENRY What are we doing tonight?

SALLY What's on TV?

HENRY There's a talk show at ten. They're interviewing a
     necrophiliac.

SALLY What?

HENRY She's being sued by the mother of a boy she violated.

SALLY Some people will do anything for money.

HENRY Are you talking about the court case or the talk show?

SALLY Both.

HENRY You want to watch it?

SALLY I'd like to know why someone would do something
     like that.

HENRY [*continuing to read*] She's in the funeral business.
     Maybe she knows your sister.

SALLY Why would you say that?

HENRY She's from the same town.

     [*Pause*]

     I'd like to meet your sister.

SALLY She's very antisocial.

HENRY Why don't you ever talk to her?

SALLY She hates me.

HENRY Why?

SALLY I don't know. When our father left she withdrew into
     herself.

HENRY How old was she?

SALLY Twelve. One day she heard our mother on the phone
     begging him to come back. She'd watch the door expecting
     him to come in at any moment. All my mother's friends

23

were divorcees. They'd sit around talking about this bastard or that bastard. Jane would sit with them. That's how she learned about men. I was older, so it didn't affect me as much.

HENRY You should get in touch with her. It's never too late.

SALLY For what?

HENRY For the healing to start.

SALLY You're beginning to sound like one of those books you read.

HENRY My last analyst told me that. She was brilliant.

SALLY Then why did you stop seeing her?

HENRY She started developing a new approach to self-help. She tried to teach people to stop looking for the hidden potential or meaning in themselves. There was no unblocking or overcoming or getting in touch. She taught people to just give up, to be happy watching TV or drinking beer. She thinks people expect too much of themselves and that they're inherently mediocre. She used to give a seminar called 'There Is Nothing Special About You'.

SALLY She does sound brilliant.

HENRY I felt she was underestimating me.

SALLY How's your new analyst?

HENRY A little scary.

SALLY Why?

HENRY I think he's preparing me for my death.

SALLY Your only problem is that you take this stuff too seriously. Why don't you get a proper job? You have too much time to sit around thinking about yourself.

HENRY I'm waiting for inspiration to strike. One day I'll find something I really want to do.

[*Pause.* SALLY *begins to cut her toenails*]

You remember when we met? Everything was new—the

art, the clothes, the music. When we went dancing they'd stop the music in the middle of the night and put on performances. Everything seemed like it was on the verge of some kind of great transformation. What happened to that intensity?

SALLY It's part of the process of maturing. We're entering a new phase in our lives. We share everything now, so there are no surprises.

[*Pause*]

HENRY You know something?

SALLY What?

HENRY I've never seen you cut your toenails before. I've seen you do everything else, but not that.

[SALLY *stands*]

Where are you going?

SALLY To bed. Come and give me a massage.

HENRY All right. I'll be up in a minute.

[SALLY *exits.* HENRY *picks up the phone and dials*]

Hello. This is Henry Booth. I'd like to volunteer for your experiment.

Scene Six

JANE *sits on a stage with a man and a woman*

CONNIE My first guest tonight is Ed Bergman. He's written a best-seller called *Unreal Estate.* Welcome to 'Talk About Us', Ed.

ED Thank you, Connie.

CONNIE Ed, you've developed a technique of arguing that can be used with great success in business, politics and even in one's personal life.

ED That's right, Connie. It's helped a lot of people achieve their goals in a very short time.

CONNIE And is it difficult to learn?

ED Not at all, Connie.

CONNIE Could you give us a demonstration?

ED Suppose you've bought my book and made a lot of money and you're arguing with someone who says wealth should be redistributed. You respond by citing a recent UN study that shows that poor people have lower rates of heart disease and cancer, eat more nutritious foods, have less overall exposure to pollution and actually have more choices in life and are happier than rich people. What can they say to that? They're stopped cold.

CONNIE And does this study exist?

ED No.

CONNIE And what about the person you're arguing with? Do they usually catch on?

ED Hardly ever, Connie. No one can know everything now. In fact, most people know next to nothing. There's just too much information. Our belief systems are patchworks of untested facts. Take this woman here. [*Indicating* JANE]

She could tell you she's an astrophysicist from Yale and that the universe is actually the size of a pea and you'd probably believe her. That's why people who can make up statistics and cite imaginary studies have a real advantage now.

CONNIE I'm not sure I follow you, Ed. Are you advocating that people lie?

ED Not at all, Connie. To lie, you have to know your facts are wrong. But when you make things up—who knows, you could be right. Some scientists at Harvard recently asked people who had no background in economics to predict movements of the Japanese stock market. And they were right 98% of the time!

CONNIE Thank you, Ed. I'm sure a lot of people will be interested in picking up your book. When we come back I'll be talking to Jane Farrel, a confessed necrophiliac.

Scene Seven

JANE You want another drink?

SALLY No thanks. It's late. I've got to drive.

JANE You can stay here if you want. I've got a double bed.
[*Pause*]
You look great. Marriage must suit you.

SALLY Really?

JANE You know, I never thought you'd last this long.

SALLY Why not?

JANE It's just against the odds. If the engines fell out of three
out of every four cars people would stop buying them.
They'd be crazy to keep buying them. But they still keep
getting married. And they say it's natural.

SALLY Well, we've survived.
[*Pause*]
Dad phoned the other night.

JANE How is he?

SALLY Fine.
[*Pause*]

JANE Is something bothering you?

SALLY No.

JANE You're very quiet tonight.

SALLY I feel like I've been talking all night.

JANE I was pretty surprised when I got your call.

SALLY I just wanted to see how you were doing.

JANE Great.
[*Pause*]
It's been a good year for me. I've never been happier.

SALLY Dad saw you on TV. So did I.

JANE What'd you think?

SALLY Didn't you think about what it would do to us?

28

JANE I needed the money.

SALLY You could have come to me.

JANE For a hundred thousand dollars? That bitch is suing me
for psychological damages.

[*Pause*]

SALLY Why don't you come and stay with me for a while?

JANE Why would I do that?

SALLY We have an extra room. You wouldn't have to pay
rent. You'd have time to look for a different job. Go back
to school. Retrain.

JANE I like my job.

SALLY No funeral home is going to hire you now.

JANE Sure they will.

SALLY Are you joking?

JANE What I do is no worse than using a live body to get off.
In fact it's better. No one gets hurt. Afterwards I can go to
the grave and mourn along with the rest of the family.

[*Pause*]

SALLY You've got to get help.

JANE There's nothing wrong with me.

SALLY Jane, please—I know why you do it.

JANE You do?

SALLY One day you're going to get in touch with your anger
at Dad and find a healthier way of expressing it.

[*Pause*]

JANE I thought you were intelligent.

SALLY Jane.

JANE You think you can talk me out of it.

SALLY I'm only trying to help.

JANE I'm very popular right now. I have plenty of guys asking
me out. More than you ever had. They think I do it because I'm hard up. They think if they screw me I'll finally

see what the real thing is and give up bodies.

SALLY What about the contact—the communication?

JANE I'm talking about something deeper than communication.

[*Pause*]

Love isn't just sharing things, good conversation, romance. That's companionship. There aren't many people who know how to love now.

[*Pause*]

If someone whips himself for love, is that sick? At least there's some feeling.

[*Pause*]

If you knew what it felt like. I find the smell of death very erotic. When you get on top of a body it tends to purge blood from the mouth ... I guess you have to be there ... You can't describe the smell of roses to someone who's never smelled anything like it.

[*Pause*]

It's late. I've got an interview tomorrow. Are you staying?

SALLY No, I think I'll go home.

JANE I could sleep on the couch. It folds out.

SALLY Henry's expecting me.

JANE Well I hope I see you again soon. Don't be a stranger.

SALLY Yes.

JANE Say hello to Mom.

SALLY I will.

[*Pause.* SALLY *turns to go*]

JANE Sally.

SALLY Yes.

JANE I know you're only trying to help. But don't worry too much about me. There's nothing you can say to change me ... It's what I like.

Scene Eight

HENRY *enters with a female* SCIENTIST. *He wears an electronic girdle and gloves covered in circuitry, and he carries a visor with headphones attached*

SCIENTIST I'm afraid the technology is a little primitive. The image will only be able to touch you in one area.

HENRY That's all right.

SCIENTIST And the touching won't always be synchronized to your movements.

HENRY It'll be like real sex then.

SCIENTIST Pardon?

HENRY It was a joke.

SCIENTIST Oh.

[*Pause*]

Is there any particular body type you like?

HENRY Voluptuous, but not fat.

[*The* SCIENTIST *begins entering* HENRY's *responses into a terminal*]

SCIENTIST Hair colour?

HENRY Blonde.

SCIENTIST Skin?

HENRY Dark.

SCIENTIST Facial features?

HENRY Big lips and eyes.

SCIENTIST Any special requests?

HENRY No.

SCIENTIST If you want to talk, the program can handle simple conversations. It has the IQ of a four year old.

HENRY All right.

[*Pause*]

31

Am I your first subject?

SCIENTIST Yes. We picked you from a field of hundreds.

HENRY Really? How did I qualify?

SCIENTIST We wanted someone of average fitness and intelligence.

HENRY Oh.

SCIENTIST Sit down, please, and I'll hook you up.

[*She begins plugging him in*]

HENRY I feel a little strange about this.

SCIENTIST Why?

HENRY It doesn't seem right somehow.

SCIENTIST Right?

HENRY Yes.

SCIENTIST Are you injuring anyone by doing this?

HENRY No.

SCIENTIST Taking advantage of anyone?

HENRY No.

SCIENTIST Are you going to cause an unwanted pregnancy or spread a social disease?

HENRY No.

SCIENTIST Then why don't you feel right?

HENRY I'm not sure. I've never had sex without a partner before.

SCIENTIST Let's face it—sex is no longer primarily for reproduction. So there's no need to have a real body there. One day we'll be able to transmit sensations directly to the brain—you'll see bodies moving and responding, feel textures and pressures, whatever the computer conjures up. And the pleasure people will feel will far surpass anything they feel in sex. It'll change the way they relate to each other. People will form bonds based on friendship rather than sex. Real physical beauty will no longer be important. Because no one can be as beautiful as an image.

HENRY My analyst says that technology can never make
people happy.

SCIENTIST Why not?

HENRY Because every new advance creates new unforeseeable
needs. He says people should learn to make do with less.

SCIENTIST Until now the world was the only reality. And it
was hard to change. In virtual reality people will be able to
change things as they please. In the real world there are
shortages, but not in the world of images. It will be the
beginning of real social change. Democracy isn't simply a
condition of free political choice. A society where everyone
can vote but where the vast majority are continually denied
the fulfilment of their desires isn't a democracy. People
won't be free until everyone can have and do exactly the
same things.

HENRY I never looked at it that way. I thought it was just sex.

SCIENTIST You're helping us bring in a new age in human
development.

HENRY I am?

SCIENTIST So relax ... It's better to have your dreams fulfilled
than analyzed.

HENRY All right. I'm ready.

[*He puts on the helmet. She starts the program*]

Hello.

[*Pause*]

Henry.

[*Pause*]

That's a pretty name.

[*Pause*]

Do you come here often?

[*Pause*]

Yes, it's a beautiful view.
[*Pause*]
Yes, I do, yes.

Scene Nine

SALLY How was your day?

HENRY Fine.

[*Pause*]

SALLY I called today. Where were you?

HENRY I went for a walk.

[*Pause*]

SALLY What are you thinking about?

HENRY Nothing.

[*Pause*]

SALLY Don't you notice anything different about me?

HENRY No.

SALLY My hair.

HENRY What about it?

SALLY I got it cut today.

HENRY Oh.

[*Pause*]

SALLY Everyone at work says it makes me look ten years younger. What do you think? Is it nice?

HENRY It ... it really suits your nose.

SALLY My nose?

HENRY Yes.

SALLY What do you mean by that?

HENRY I don't know.

SALLY Is my nose that big?

HENRY No.

SALLY Then why did you say that about my nose?

HENRY I don't know. I couldn't think of anything else to say.

[*Pause*]

SALLY I'm worried about you, Henry.

HENRY Why?

SALLY You say things that don't have anything to do with what we're talking about. You haven't shaved for days. Can you remember the last time we made love? Why can't you be happy with what you have?

HENRY I am happy.

SALLY Then why do you keep volunteering for those experiments?

HENRY I'm helping advance the boundaries of science.

SALLY I preferred it when you were into Buddhism.

HENRY I don't believe in all that denial now.

SALLY Why not?

HENRY Because there's no reason for it. Soon people will have everything they want.

SALLY It seems so childish—wanting to have and touch everything. There are more important things than sex.

HENRY It's not just sex.

SALLY It is sex!

[Pause]

When I was younger, my roommate invited a man whose wife was out of town over to our apartment for the evening. We had a wonderful dinner, with lots of wine, and afterwards we all lay down near each other to listen to some music. Before long my roommate said she was falling asleep and went into her bedroom. Her friend asked if he could stay until the song was over. As we lay there listening I felt the most beautiful sensation rising through my body. There was nothing I wanted more than to reach over and take his hand. And I knew he wanted to touch me too. But he couldn't. So we lay there thinking about each other until the music ended.

[Pause]

I used to think it was a tragedy that nothing happened. But

looking back I'm glad it didn't. How could our touching
have made any difference? It wouldn't have added anything
to what we felt. It would only have cheapened a beautiful
memory.

[*Pause*]

Just be with me,Henry. Please. I'm right here ... You don't
need anything more.

HENRY You're right.

[*He kisses her*]

Scene Ten

HENRY *lies sleeping on a chair.* JANE *stands over him*

JANE Hello.

> [HENRY *wakes up and looks at* JANE. *He reaches up and*
> *touches her face, then looks at his hand*]
> Do you always greet people this way?

HENRY Who are you?

JANE Jane.

HENRY How did you get in here?

JANE [*holding up a key*] Through the door.

> [*Pause*]
> Where's Sally?

HENRY You know Sally?

JANE She's my sister.

HENRY I saw you on TV.

JANE What did you think?

HENRY You were wonderful.

> [*Pause*]
> I felt I understood you. It must be hard.

JANE What's hard?

HENRY Being different. Wanting something different.

JANE I'm not different. I'm normal.

> [*Pause*]
> It's other people that have the problem.
> [*Pause. She picks up a statue of the Buddha*]
> Is this yours?

HENRY Yes.

JANE Are you religious?

HENRY A little.

JANE A little?

HENRY I've read the Buddhist scriptures.

JANE My father was religious. He used to say no to everything without thinking.

HENRY Sally is very religious.

JANE Sally is a prude.

[*Pause*]

I don't understand her. You grow up with someone. You sleep in the same bed. You share all their secrets. And you still don't know anything about them.

HENRY She's very fond of you.

JANE She hates me.

[*Pause*]

HENRY Will you be staying long?

JANE No. I'm on my way to a psychiatric hospital.

[*Pause*]

They settled my case. The woman dropped the charges.

HENRY That's good.

JANE Yes.

HENRY Did she realize how ridiculous it was?

JANE She didn't want me to join her son.

HENRY You threatened to kill yourself?

JANE I did kill myself.

[*Pause*]

They brought me back.

[*Pause*]

They've recommended a hospital.

HENRY They'll help you.

JANE I doubt it. The more they try to convince me I'm doing something wrong, the more I want it ... Everything seems so insignificant by comparision.

[*Pause*]

HENRY I'd like to show you something.

[*He exits and returns with a box*]
It's something I bought for Sally.
[*He pulls a body suit and visor out of the box*]

JANE What is it?

HENRY It allows you to see and touch a computer-generated body ... You should try it.

JANE Why?

HENRY It would solve your problems.

JANE I don't have a problem.

HENRY No one would care what you did. You can't commit a crime with an image.

JANE No thanks.

HENRY Why not?

JANE It seems a little weird.

HENRY Weird?

JANE It just wouldn't be the same.

[*Pause*]

I'm afraid I have to go.

HENRY You just got here.

JANE There's a train at five.

HENRY Sally should be home soon.

JANE Tell her I'll call.

HENRY It's too bad she won't see you.

[*Pause*]

It was nice meeting you.

JANE Take good care of Sally.

Scene Eleven

SALLY *and* HENRY *lie listening to music*

SALLY I don't understand.

HENRY What?

SALLY Why she left five minutes after she got here.

HENRY Are we going to worry about this all night? I thought
we were going to have a romantic evening.

SALLY She might do something crazy.

HENRY She's at a hospital.

SALLY What hospital?

HENRY I don't know.

[*Pause*]

SALLY Did you do something to drive her away?

HENRY No.

SALLY Did you say anything?

HENRY No.

SALLY You must have done something.

HENRY I just showed her your present.

SALLY What present?

HENRY I was going to wait for the right moment.

[*He exits and returns with the box.* SALLY *turns off the
music*]

SALLY What is it?

HENRY [*pulling out two body suits*] It's going to make us rich.
It's an interactive system. It allows two people to make love
even when they're miles apart.

[*He hands her a visor*]

Try it on.

SALLY Why?

HENRY It'll make me look better. It enhances my features.

SALLY I like the way you look.

HENRY Try it. Put the suit on too.

SALLY No.

HENRY Why not?

SALLY I don't want to make love to a machine.

HENRY You'll be making love to me.

SALLY How could it be you?

HENRY We never see or touch the real person.

SALLY I do.

HENRY You see something created by your brain. So what does it matter if we adjust the perceiving mechanisms. It'll be me responding. Haven't you ever wanted to be more beautiful?

SALLY No.

HENRY You could look the way you did ten years ago.

SALLY No!

[*Pause*]

You're planning to market these things?

HENRY Think of all the people who feel they've been cheated by life. I'm going to give them a means to be happy. It'll be the beginning of real social change.

SALLY What?

HENRY It'll be the beginning of democracy!

SALLY Democracy?

HENRY Yes.

SALLY You're not a prophet, Henry—you're a pimp. You'll be selling more sexist consumerism.

HENRY It's not just sex. One day we'll fly, sound the ocean, scatter ourselves across the universe—all without moving. If you knew what it felt like! We could visit Indra's Grove! We could experience it together.

[*Pause*]

SALLY Am I that ugly?

HENRY You're beautiful.

Scene Twelve

SALLY *sits in an office with a male* DOCTOR

DOCTOR Thank you for coming. I think you can help us with your sister's treatment.

SALLY We've never been close.

DOCTOR She needs you.

SALLY Do you think you can cure her?

DOCTOR We don't try to cure people here. To cure them we'd have to know what they ought to want. We simply try to help them find acceptable substitutes.

SALLY Substitutes?

DOCTOR We've found that aversion therapy doesn't really work. Lately we've been having some success with virtual reality. If we make the experience readily available, the desire tends to abate somewhat. We hope to get your sister back at her old job. I'd like you to visit every week if possible—there's no substitute for human contact—but remember, please don't be judgmental.

SALLY All right.

DOCTOR I'm afraid I have to go. She should be here in a moment.

SALLY Do you mind if I ask you a question?

DOCTOR I'm very busy. If you'd like to make an appointment ...

SALLY My husband and I have separated.

DOCTOR I'm sorry but ...

SALLY I can't seem to relate to people any more. I haven't been out in weeks. I feel boring and unattractive.

DOCTOR You're very attractive. And I'm sure ...

SALLY I don't know if it's me or everyone else. It's something I've noticed lately. Everyone is so preoccupied. Whenever people talk to me I get the feeling they're just being polite. They're dying to get somewhere else. They talk to me just long enough not to seem rude. All the time they're only half there—I can see it in their eyes—they're thinking about ... Are you listening to me?

DOCTOR Yes, of course. You seem like a very interesting person.

SALLY In what way?

DOCTOR In what way?

SALLY Yes.

DOCTOR I'm just getting to know you.

SALLY Then how do you know I'm interesting?

DOCTOR Because everyone is interesting in their own way. You should be proud of yourself.

SALLY Why?

DOCTOR Because you know something no one else knows.

SALLY What's that?

DOCTOR What it's like to be you ... I'm afraid I have to go.

[*He exits.* JANE *enters*]

JANE [*calling*] Doctor! Doctor!

SALLY He's very busy.

JANE He sees you more than me. Maybe you have the problem.

SALLY Maybe I do.

[*Pause*]

JANE How's Henry?

SALLY We agreed to separate for a month.

JANE It's probably better for you.

SALLY Haven't you ever wanted to be with someone?

JANE No. I could never adjust. How can you stand it?

SALLY When you get in a bath the water is a different temperature than the skin. The whole beauty is in letting the heat flow into the body. That's what it's like when you meet someone. You feel the other person flowing into you, warming you.

JANE Until the whole thing is lukewarm.

[*Pause*]

You must have better things to do. You don't have to stay.

SALLY It's all right. I wanted to see how you were doing.

JANE I'm fine.

[*Pause*]

SALLY Have you made any friends here?

JANE No. Everyone is crazy here. I'm hoping if I play along they'll let me have my old job back.

SALLY You could stay with me.

JANE I don't think it would work.

SALLY I just want you to be happy.

JANE These are the best years of my life.

SALLY Why do you say that?

JANE Because I have nothing to lose. My life isn't worth anything now.

SALLY Jane …

JANE Everything is so special now—so vivid. The other day in the park a couple stopped to talk to me. I was almost crying when I petted their dog. They looked at me like— My God, haven't you ever seen a dog before? When you're in one place for so long, you watch all the changes in the world, and you feel you won't be able to adjust if you get back out there, that you won't know how to act or live.

SALLY You've only been here seven days.

[*Pause*]

JANE I'm tired. I think you should go.

SALLY I'm sorry—I'm not feeling very well. My marriage is finished.

[*Pause*]

I brought you some food.

JANE Thanks.

SALLY I wasn't sure what you'd want. So I brought an assortment.

JANE I appreciate it.

SALLY I'm sorry our last visit wasn't so good. I'd like to get to know you ... Should I stay?

JANE Yes. Please.

Scene Thirteen

[SALLY *sits at a café table.* HENRY *walks past, then returns*]

HENRY Sally?

SALLY Henry?

HENRY I thought it was you.

SALLY What are you doing here?

HENRY Business. What about you?

SALLY I moved here two months ago. To be near Jane.

HENRY [*indicating the extra chair*] Are you expecting anyone?

SALLY No.

HENRY Mind if I join you?

SALLY No.

   [*He sits*]

HENRY You look great. It's good to see you. I love your hair.

SALLY How's business?

HENRY Great—I just got back from the Himalayas.

SALLY What?

HENRY We're exporting to some of the monasteries there.
The monks have adapted very quickly to the technology.

SALLY What do they do with it?

HENRY Simulate past lives.

   [*Pause*]

I was thinking about you the other day ... I found one of
your toenails. When I was cleaning. For some reason I
started to cry. It brought back so many memories.

SALLY Did you keep it?

HENRY I would have, but it seemed like a strange thing to do.

   [*Pause*]

Are you seeing anyone?

SALLY No.

HENRY Why not?

SALLY My work keeps me busy. And I spend a lot of time
with Jane.

[*Pause*]

I bought a dog. We go for long walks in the park. In the
morning there's a beautiful mist. He's happy chasing sticks
or sniffing in the grass. He loves it when I scratch his back,
just below his collar. He's very easily satisfied.

[*Pause*]

I should go. He hasn't been walked today.

HENRY There's something I should tell you.

SALLY What?

HENRY I'm seeing someone.

SALLY A person?

HENRY Yes. Of course.

[*Pause*]

I felt I should tell you.

SALLY It's really got nothing to do with me. You don't need
my permission.

[*Pause*]

HENRY It's very serious.

SALLY Does she know you were married?

HENRY He.

SALLY What?

HENRY I met him at a sales conference.

SALLY You're gay?

HENRY No.

SALLY Henry, please, we're old enough to ...

HENRY When we make love he's not a man. We use a computer.

[*Pause*]

I'm still attracted to women. But he understands me.

[*Shadows of trees moving in the wind fall across the table.*

The sound of birds and rustling leaves]
We're still working things out. It's not perfect but we both feel it's worth pursuing. We can overlook the trivial differences.

[*Pause*]

Do you ever think about me?

SALLY Yes—but only about the irrelevant things.

HENRY Like what?

SALLY Your eyes, your voice, the way you touched me.

[*Pause*]

HENRY One day we'll all be pulses of light or clouds of energy. No one will suffer from hunger or cold or loss or sorrow. We'll feel pleasure every moment of our lives. We'll know why we're alive and how to make each other happy.

SALLY I've got to walk my dog.

[*Pause*]

Good bye, Henry.

HENRY Here's my card. Keep in touch.

SALLY I will.

[*She exits. A celestial nymph enters and sits beside* HENRY]

HENRY Do you mind if we just talk tonight?

WOMAN No.

Scene Fourteen

JANE *applies make-up to a corpse.* MARK *stands nearby*

MARK You've made him look beautiful. I don't know how
you do it.
[*Pause*]
It's a lost art. These new funeral homes are going to put us
out of business. No one wants to see dead bodies any more.
Not when they can see their loved ones in the flesh.
[*Pause*]
Want me to walk you home?

JANE No thanks. I'll be a while still.
[*Pause*]

MARK I don't know if you heard—I'm married.

JANE Congratulations.

MARK It happened pretty quickly. I met her at a party. We hit
it off right away. Ended up talking the whole night. She's a
recovering alcoholic, but she's a great communicator. She
can remember poems that she learned sitting at university
when she wants to recite them. We'd love to have you over
for dinner some time.

JANE That would be nice.

MARK I had quite a scare this morning. When I woke up and
looked at the time it was ten o'clock. I couldn't figure out
why the alarm hadn't gone off. I picked up the phone to
call my wife at work and I couldn't get a dial tone. All of a
sudden I realized I wasn't hearing anything. I was deaf!
Turns out I had green fluid in my ears. It took the doctor
two hours to drain them.
[*Pause*]
Remember the time you told me to shut up?

JANE Yes. I'm sorry. I wasn't feeling very well.

MARK That's all right. I didn't take it personally. My wife says
I never talk about anything important. I go home and tell
her about my day. She says, tell me about your real feel-
ings. I say—these *are* my real feelings!
[*Pause*]
We were sorry to hear about your problem.

JANE I'm better now.

MARK That's good.

JANE I woke up one day and I was cured. The things I wanted
didn't seem important any more.

MARK Well, we're glad to have you back.
[*Pause*]

JANE This morning I bought a donut.

MARK A donut?

JANE Yes.
[*Pause*]

MARK Well that's good.

JANE Everything smelled so good in the store. They had them
lined up in boxes, row after row. There were so many to
choose from, it took me a long time to decide. Finally, I
picked a chocolate one.

MARK Really?

JANE When the woman at the counter saw what I had, she
pointed at some chocolate eclairs and said—If you like
that, you'll love these! As if one thing followed from the
other!
[*She laughs.* MARK *stares at her*]

MARK Well, she must have had quite a sense of humour.
[*Pause*]
I can tell you're feeling better. That's the first time I've seen
you laugh.

[*Pause*]

My wife's expecting me. You'll lock up?

JANE Yes.

MARK Have a good night.

JANE Thanks.

[MARK *exits.* JANE *continues to work on the corpse.* SALLY *enters*]

SALLY Who was that?

JANE A friend.

SALLY I'm going for a walk. Want to come?

JANE All right.

SALLY I ran into Henry.

JANE How is he?

SALLY It's hard to say. He's seeing a man now. I'm not sure he's any happier than when he was with me. He's still talking about the future.

JANE Some people just don't know what they don't want.

SALLY [*laughing*] Yes … How long will you be?

JANE Five minutes.

SALLY I don't know how you can stand it in here. It's so cold. And the smell … I'll never understand you.

[*She kisses her*]

I'll see you upstairs.

JANE Yes.

[SALLY *exits.* JANE *continues to apply make-up to the corpse. After a moment she looks at the corpse and smoothes its hair back. She pulls the sheet up over its face. The lights fade slowly as she stares at the corpse*]

John Mighton's plays include *Scientific Americans*, *Possible Worlds* and *A Short History of Night*, which was awarded the Governor General's Award for Drama in 1992. He lectured in philosophy at McMaster University and is currently completing a Ph.D. in Mathematics at the University of Toronto.

Editor for the Press: Jason Sherman
Cover Design: Christopher Wadsworth / Reactor

For a list of our drama titles, or to receive a
catalogue, write to:

Coach House Press
50 Prince Arthur Avenue, Suite 107
Toronto, Canada M5R 1B5